the little
book of
humanist
funerals

the little book of humanist funerals

Remembering and
celebrating a life

**Andrew Copson and
Alice Roberts**

with Zena Birch,
Deborah Hooper,
and the celebrants
of Humanists UK

PIATKUS

First published in Great Britain in 2023 by Piatkus

10 9 8 7 6 5 4 3

Text copyright © British Humanist Association 2023

The moral right of the authors has been asserted.

A CIP catalogue record for this book is available from
the British Library.

ISBN 978-0-349-43405-6

Designed and typeset by EM&EN
Printed and bound in Great Britain by Clays Ltd, Elcograf S.p.A

Papers used by Piatkus are from well-managed forests
and other responsible sources.

PIATKUS
An imprint of
Little, Brown Book Group
Carmelite House
50 Victoria Embankment
London EC4Y 0DZ

An Hachette UK Company
www.hachette.co.uk

Contents

Welcome

Death is the inevitable end to every life. Everybody you know will die someday, and so will you.

We can't ignore the inevitability of death, and indeed, for many humanists, it is the finite length of a human life that gives it meaning.

Human beings are not the sort of animals to which events just happen. We have a deep need to understand those events, to give them meaning and shape, through the stories we tell ourselves about our lives.

Archaeology shows us how, long before the written word was invented, people felt the need to mark the end of a life with ceremony of some kind.

All rituals and ceremonies are based on beliefs and values, whether we realise and acknowledge them or not. Funeral ceremonies are based on our most fundamental beliefs about life and death – and the meaning and purpose of existence.

The humanist approach is that we have one life, and death is the end of that life. It makes sense to enjoy your life and the things that give it meaning – relationships, worthwhile projects, simple pleasures, the beauty of nature and the arts, curiosity, creativity, love.

A humanist funeral is a non-religious ceremony that reflects this understanding, while also being inclusive and welcoming those with religious beliefs. It also reflects the fact that every human life is utterly unique. Humanist funerals are completely personal and wholly focussed on the life of the person who has died and the needs of those who knew them and loved them.

This little book is not a 'how to' guide for arranging a humanist funeral, but it will help you to start thinking about the ideas, beliefs, and values that will inform a funeral, whether that's yours or someone else's.

It is also an invitation to think about mortality – and the sort of questions that we often put to the back of our minds. Anyone who wants to live with their eyes open to reality has to come to terms with death. In doing so, we can learn to live more fully and make sure, when the end comes, the story of our life has been a good one.

Andrew Copson and Alice Roberts
December 2022

Introduction

Non-religious funerals and memorial services have been around for a long time, despite many people thinking that they are a modern concept: Humanists UK has been providing humanist funerals since 1896, creating memorable and meaningful ceremonies for non-religious people who want to mark death with dignity, without reference to an afterlife.

Today, with over half of the population identifying as non-religious since the 2018 British Social Attitudes Survey, more than a million people each year attend a humanist ceremony, and humanist funerals are increasingly the preferred choice for families who want to commemorate their loved one as a unique and valued individual, with no religion.

The Humanist Ceremonies network of celebrants, trained and accredited by Humanists UK, operates throughout England, Wales, Northern Ireland, and the Channel Islands. Each celebrant is independent and self-employed, but works collegiately with shared values and commitment to serving families who seek non-religious ceremonies to mark the most important moments in their lives.

Through rigorous training, professional development and peer review, celebrants are able to work thoughtfully, sensitively and flexibly with families to create a funeral ceremony for their loved one in exactly the way they wish.

The majority of humanist funerals take place in crematoria or cemeteries but they can be held anywhere and at any time, with the coffin present or as a memorial or ashes ceremony, in a hotel, pub room or village hall, or outdoors, in woodlands or on the beach. Humanist funerals are warm and inclusive, welcoming to all, regardless of belief or faith, and very often there will be a moment of reflection within the ceremony, where those who wish can make a silent prayer.

People sometimes ask whether or not religious content can be included in a humanist funeral. The answer is: if the person who has died was not religious, then the celebrant can always find a way to create an appropriate and authentic humanist ceremony for them. What is key is that the most solemn and significant moment of the ceremony, the farewell (what might be called the committal in a traditional funeral) is not a religious one. We are not sending the person who has died to an afterlife: the ceremony recognises that their one life is over, and they have become part of the eternal cycle of nature, their atoms and energy forever around us. Although as humanist celebrants we won't lead an act of collective worship, we recognise that, culturally, religion is embedded in our everyday lives, and also that many non-religious people appreciate the beauty of music and literature with religious influences. We understand, too, that families are diverse and varied in their beliefs – after all, we all have families ourselves, and know that it may be important for this to be reflected. So a humanist funeral could include a favourite hymn, when it's a reminder of a rugby club, for example, or a poem with a religious reference because it was a favourite at school. If it's significant to one close family member for a prayer to be included, it would be inauthentic (and meaningless) for the celebrant to read it, but if someone else is able to do so then it can be part of the ceremony. The celebrant will always work with the family to find a solution.

A humanist funeral is not always the easiest choice for a bereaved family in deep grief. In my role as a celebrant, I often say to the families I work with that the planning of the ceremony – recounting memories, choosing readings and pieces of music, approving the script I have drafted – may ask a lot of them at what might be the most difficult of times. These can all feel like additional tasks when there are already a great many other onerous admin jobs around the death of their person to be completed. But, for most families, the meeting with their celebrant is an extremely positive experience, a chance to come together and collectively remember and share family stories, perhaps the first time ever they have done so. They are often very emotional gatherings, with laughter as well as tears, and families frequently say how helpful they have been in the process of grieving.

In the end, what the celebrant and the family do together is create a totally unique and personal ceremony for the person who has died, authentic, honest, and meaningful to everyone present. The family can take comfort in knowing that they have done their very best to say a final farewell to their person in the most fitting way they can.

Deborah Hooper
Director of Ceremonies
December 2022

The role of a celebrant

Nobody wants to be at a funeral. Who wouldn't rather be having a cup of tea, a dance, or even an argument with the person who died? But then, too many people haven't been to a *good* funeral – one where they came away invigorated with gratitude and love for the person they knew, or quietly healing and soothed by the closing of a difficult chapter, or simply involved in a ceremony that did what was needed.

Our role as humanist funeral celebrants is to make the funeral ceremony as (appropriately) brilliant as it can be. For it to encapsulate grief and shock, but also laughter and love. For it to reflect the idiosyncrasies and complexities which are part of every relationship. And all of this not in spite of the circumstances, but because of the circumstances. All of us deserve a good funeral.

Sometimes it's easy to celebrate a life, but there are many circumstances where it's hard. Whatever the situation, it will be deftly handled by your humanist funeral celebrant. Your work with a celebrant will be personal, tailored to your requirements, and full of everything necessary to reflect the personality of the deceased.

Your celebrant will learn all about the life and character of the person who has died. They will meet with you and whoever else is needed. They will support you in choosing between a graveside ceremony, a crematorium, a woodland burial, a celebration of life at a later date, or any of the myriad options available to you. They will help you choose music, guide you through rituals and symbolic gestures, liaise with any funeral directors, help you find readings, and find ways to include others. They will start the storytelling and memory sharing that will spill out and live long beyond the ceremony. They will support your wishes, and help find what feels best for you.

The second funeral I ever conducted was a celebration of life for a dear friend. It was tough: 48 hours before the ceremony, I had dozens of anecdotes, but I hadn't been able to write a single word. I found myself in an unusual panic. Why couldn't I write anything? I realised I was angry. My feelings were getting in the way, and I realised that would be how everyone gathered felt. So, I addressed this from the start.

As we gathered on a clifftop for the ceremony it seemed fitting to shout our rage into the open sky. By openly admitting how much we didn't want to be there, and by collectively shouting 'SCREW

CANCER' out over the sea and beyond, something astonishing happened. We felt communed, heard, oddly soothed in our collective rage. It cleared the space for us to be able to then remember our friend properly: in her brilliant, irreverent, celebratory, all-dancing way.

This is not right for all ceremonies. But it was right for her.

My *first* funeral came about because the person who died knew I would let a mariachi band play live, in full regalia, in the crematorium chapel. One of her last requests was for people to leave her with her favourite live music ringing around their ears.

This is not right for all ceremonies. But it was right for her.

Your celebrant will help you find whatever is right to honour the individual person who has died.

A humanist funeral is, at its heart, a reflection of a humanist approach to life. It is full of humanity and what it means to be alive.

Zena Birch
December 2022

DEATH AND LIFE

There are only two days of less than 24 hours in our lifetime – sitting like bookends astride our lives. One is celebrated every year and the other makes us see living as precious.

Kathryn Mannix

Being dead

We are such stuff
As dreams are made on; and our little life
Is rounded with a sleep

William Shakespeare

Being dead shouldn't be something to worry about.

Close your eyes and think back over your life so far. What is your earliest memory? Perhaps you can just about remember an early birthday or a first play-mate. Try to think back further, as far as you can.

Now try to think how you felt before you were born.

Maybe that's too much of a stretch. Try instead to think about how it feels when you're asleep. Not the moments when you're half awake or dreaming. Think about how you feel during dreamless sleep. Or if you've ever been under a general anaesthetic, try to remember how you felt then.

The point is, of course, that you can't remember these things – neither unconsciousness, nor the years before your birth.

Look back on the eternity that passed before we were born and consider how it counts as absolutely nothing to us. This is a mirror, held up for us by Nature, that shows how it will be after we are dead. Is there anything frightening in this sight? Anything depressing? Anything that is not more restful than the deepest of sleeps?

Lucretius

In the past, people didn't know that thinking occurred in our brains. Some people believed it was possible that the part of us that thought, and looked out at the world, was separate from our body.

Now we know that is not the case. You aren't living in your body – you *are* your body. The human mind is an extraordinary phenomenon, but we know from neuroscience and psychology that the mind is what the brain *does*. It is not a separate 'soul'. Your personality matures and changes just as your body grows and changes and there is no essence of you, no separate 'soul' that could exist away from your body and brain.

No one will ever know what it is like to be dead because, once we are dead, we cease to be.

Being dead is nothing to fear.

I was not and was conceived.

I loved, and did a little work.

I am not, and grieve not.

W K Clifford

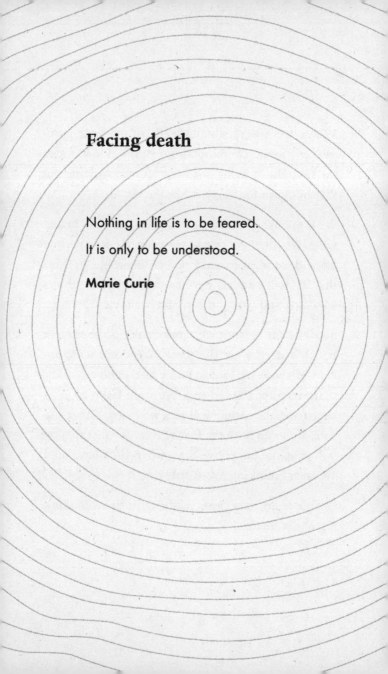

Facing death

Nothing in life is to be feared.
It is only to be understood.

Marie Curie

When we worry about death or – more commonly – avoid thinking about it, it is not so much the thought of being dead that we are avoiding but the thought of no longer being *alive*.

We don't like the idea that our lives may end before we have done the things we want to do. We love life and we want to carry on. We don't like to think that we will one day have to stop doing the things we enjoy and seeing the people we love.

Some of the reasons we avoid thinking about other people's deaths are the same. We don't want the lives of those we love to come to an end any more than we want ours to end. We want them to carry on having the same pleasures we enjoy. Other reasons are to do with the fear of loss. We fear that we will miss the people we love when they have died. We avoid thinking about that too.

But there are very good reasons not to avoid thinking about death.

Death destroys a person,

but the idea of death

saves them . . .

E M Forster

Death is natural. Without it there would be no life.

For a word to be spoken,

there must be silence . . .

Before, and after.

Ursula K. Le Guin

Nature's law is that

all things change and turn,

and pass away, so that in

due course, different things

may be.

Marcus Aurelius

Death is essential for there to be any meaning in our lives at all.

It is the fact of death that brings structure to our lives. It frames our existence on this earth. Without death, but with the prospect of eternal life instead, what could motivate us to do anything, to care for others, to seek achievements – what would be the point?

Without death, nothing we do would have any value or enjoyment.

A sentence is not finished till it has a full stop, and every life needs a dying to complete it. It is dying that finishes us, that ends our story. When the map of our life is complete, and we die in the richness of our history, some among the living will miss us for a while, but the earth will go on without us. Its day is longer than ours, though we now know that it too will die. Our brief finitude Is but a beautiful spark in the vast darkness of space. So we should live the fleeting day with passion and, when the night comes, depart from it with grace.

Richard Holloway

Even if you avoid thinking about death, it is still going to happen – to you and to everyone else. However you feel about it, death is still a fact, and reality is always better faced than avoided.

Dying is a natural consequence of living and we must come to terms with it if we want to live well. When you honestly reconcile yourself to death, you can find the greatest peace, deepest resilience, and most authentic meaning a human can know.

Andrew Copson

Be brave in the face of death. Be sad at leaving but don't let these be your final emotions. Let it be gratitude for the life you had.

Clive James

There is no end to the adventures that we can have if only we seek them with our eyes open.

Jawaharlal Nehru

If we come to terms with our own mortality, it can help us appreciate the limited time we really have and motivate us to make the most of the opportunities our lives may offer. We become more likely to pursue our ambitions, cherish our relationships, and make meaningful decisions and choices.

I throw everything I have

into living as much as

I possibly can, for if this is

the only life we have

it makes sense to try

as much as possible to

live life to the absolute full.

Stephen Fry

Imagine you are listening to a favourite piece of music. You're enjoying it. Maybe you're humming or singing along, tapping your foot, perhaps dancing a little. Then, just when the track is about to end, it skips back to the beginning and starts again. That's okay a few times, as it's one of your favourites after all. But it happens again. Then again. In fact it never stops, the track never changes, and you are listening to it again and again and again, constantly on a loop.

Or imagine you're eating your favourite food. The anticipation and then that first mouthful – delicious! Then the second mouthful and the whole thing a real treat from start to finish. Only there is no finish. The dish is always full and you're always eating.

On and on and on.

How long before your once favourite song is meaningless to you? How long before your once favourite treat becomes tasteless, maybe even makes you sick to your stomach?

Or imagine you are reading a novel or watching a great movie. The characters are engaging, their relationships twist and turn and are full of interest. You can't wait to see how they turn out in the end. But there is no end. The story just goes on and on. It never ends. There is no resolution.

Our own lives are a story, as are the lives of everyone we know. They need to end for them to make sense.

Fear of death is natural. Death represents the end of our existence and for most people this is not something to be completely welcomed.

But death is a natural part of life and we can all find ways, and can support each other, to cope with our fears. Human beings are psychologically strong enough to do this and have the ability to articulate and discuss our feelings about it.

Funerals can be an important part of processing and understanding death. In many humanist funeral ceremonies, something will be said about facing and accepting the fact of death, what it is and what it means.

This is not just so we can make sense of what has happened to the person who has died, but so we can make sense together of what death means to us all and how we can come to terms with it.

You can cry about death and very properly so, your own as well as anybody else's. But it's inevitable, so you'd better grapple with it and cope and be aware that not only is it inevitable, but it has always been inevitable.

David Attenborough

By facing up to death, we can find the peace that comes from acceptance. Death, whether it is the death of others, or our own imminent death, can create great feelings of personal loss. Grief is painful and destabilising. Learning to accept the reality of death will make us more able to survive tragedies and to heal in due course – even though we may always bear the scars.

The ancient school of Stoic philosophy encouraged us to think about the deaths of those we love before they happen. We should treat each encounter with those we love as if it is the last we will ever have, and take time to realise that we may never see them again. The idea was that by picturing this future reality, we will build resilience for when it happens.

Ever since I found out that earthworms have
    taste buds
all over the delicate pink strings of their bodies,
I pause dropping apple peels into the compost bin,
    imagine
the dark, writhing ecstasy, the sweetness of apples
permeating their pores. I offer beets and parsley,
avocado, and melon, the feathery tops of carrots.
I'd always thought theirs a menial life, eyeless
    and hidden,
almost vulgar — though now, it seems, they bear
    a pleasure
so sublime, so decadent, I want to contribute
    however I can,
forgetting, a moment, my place on the menu.

Danusha Laméris

The fact that we do not know when we are going to die or how can be a source of anxiety if we are not at peace with it. By accepting that a large part of this is outside of our control, we can remind ourselves of that fact when worries encroach on us, and realise that the only thing we have control over is whether to worry or not.

We cannot escape death,

but we can escape

the fear of it.

Epictetus

One of the other ways to defeat fear is through knowledge. If we learn more about what happens to bodies after death, we might learn to see it not as repulsive or fearful but as natural.

Throughout our lives, all of our cells work hard to keep our body up and running. When we die, the processes of life in each cell cease, and our bodies begin to disintegrate. This is the same for every living being on the planet: every single animal, plant, fungus and single-celled organism dies, decomposes and their molecules and atoms are recycled to form other things. We are part of that cycle of life and death.

If we can come to terms with that, we can begin to make our own conscious choices about what we want the fate of our physical remains to be.

Do we want to be cremated, buried, or something else? Today a wide variety of options are possible. Our choices may be guided by tradition, by cost, or by concern for the environment.

I will leave a sum in my last will for my body to be carried to Brazil and to these forests. It will be laid out in a manner secure against the possums and the vultures just as we make our chickens secure; and this great Coprophanaeus beetle will bury me. They will enter, will bury, will live on my flesh; and in the shape of their children and mine, I will escape death. No worm for me nor sordid fly, I will buzz in the dusk like a huge bumble bee. I will be many, buzz even as a swarm of motorbikes, be borne, body by flying body out into the Brazilian wilderness beneath the stars, lofted under those beautiful and un-fused elytra which we will all hold over our backs. So finally I too will shine like a violet ground beetle under a stone.

Bill Hamilton

Humans also make sense of things by putting them into words and sharing those words. Having conversations, whether with those closest to us or with professional counsellors and therapists, about what death is and how we feel about it can help us to reduce fear and increase our ability to deal with difficult situations involving death.

Dying Matters is a campaign led by the charity Hospice UK, which encourages people to talk more about death, dying and bereavement.

Its mission is to break the stigma, challenge preconceptions and normalise public openness around these topics.

Its website has resources and links to help us all be more open.

www.dyingmatters.org

Humanist funerals are honest about the fact of death. It is the end of an individual life.

But humanist funerals also recognise that death does not leave us inconsolable.

Let us be honest with death.
Let us not pretend that it is less than it is.
It is separation. It is sorrow. It is grief.
But let us neither pretend that death is more
    than it is.
It is not annihilation.
As long as memory endures, his influence
    will be felt. It is not an end to love –
humanity's need for love from each of us
    is boundless.
It is not an end to joy and laughter –
nothing would less honour one so vibrant
than to make our lives drab in counterfeit
    respect!
Let us be honest with death, for in that
    honesty
we will understand him better
and ourselves more deeply.

A. Powell Davies

Life after death

In the Ramtop Village they believe that no-one is finally dead until the ripples they cause in the world die away, until the clock he wound up winds down – until the wine she made has finished its ferment, until the crop they planted is harvested. The span of someone's life, they say, is only the core of their actual existence.

Terry Pratchett

There is no physical life after death but people do live on in other ways.

The most obvious way that people can live on is in the memories of those who knew them. You will hold memories of people you loved and were close to, and you may continue to carry their perspectives with you. You will also remember the lives of people you didn't know personally but whose actions were influential or inspirational. In this way, everyone contributes to the culture that is passed on from generation to generation.

The choices and actions made by people who have died live on through their influence on the living.

So this is where the dead go in our imaginations: they continue to live with us in the moments when we are sad and terrified. They cheer for us. They give us unbelievable strength and the courage we lack to carry on in situations. They coax us through. They lead us where we need to be, to experience the joy and capability that was them. They who have been with us in life, manage to teach us how and where in death, we can listen for them and find their voices and their essence, once again.

Anakana Schofield

When we are remembering people, we are keeping alive not just the person we knew just before their death, but the person we knew at different times throughout their life.

It can be particularly comforting for those who have known a person whose condition and quality of life has deteriorated for us to be able to remember them as they once were.

Remember me as I used to be
Not as you saw me last.
Recall the days of happy times
Spent with me in the past.
Instead of tears for what might have been
Smile for all that we shared.
A life so full of happiness made so, because
    you cared.
And next time you see a rose in bloom
Or hear a blackbird's song.
Remember me as I used to be
In the days when I was strong.
I would not wish for you to grieve
For the person I had become
Instead relive those memories, of the days
    when I was young.
So remember me as I used to be
Not as you saw me last.
And keep me close in memory
In your present and in our past.

Anonymous

Epitaph

When I die
Give what's left of me away
To children
And old men that wait to die.
And if you need to cry,
Cry for your brother
Walking the street beside you.
And when you need me,
Put your arms
Around anyone
And give them
What you need to give to me.
I want to leave you something,
Something better
Than words
Or sounds.

Look for me
In the people I've known
Or loved,
And if you cannot give me away,
At least let me live on in your eyes
And not your mind.
You can love me most
By letting
Hands touch hands,
By letting bodies touch bodies,
And by letting go
Of children
That need to be free.
Love doesn't die,
People do.
So, when all that's left of me
Is love,
Give me away.

Merrit Malloy

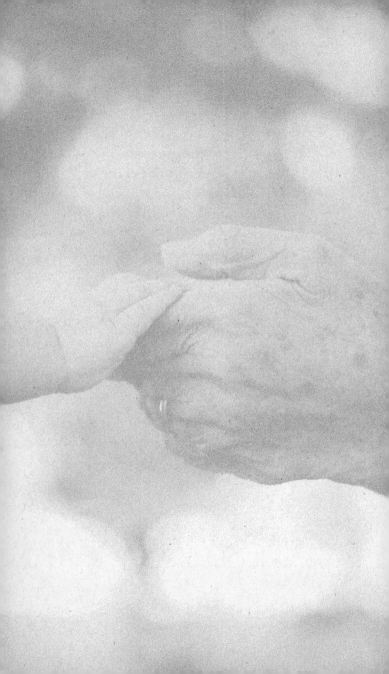

Even if nothing concrete has been handed down, that isn't to say that an individual has left no trace of her existence. A look, a gesture transmitted from parent to child, a way of dressing, a song sung by a bedside may travel down the generations. It's an intangible legacy but a very real one. Perhaps a child of today might stand next to her great-great-great-grandmother and reveal their kinship in a turn of phrase. They who are not forgotten are not dead.

Helen Dunmore

To die completely,

a person must not only

forget but be forgotten,

and he who is not forgotten

is not dead.

Samuel Butler

Living well for a humanist is about seeking fulfil-ment and helping others to do the same.

In life, the connections and relationships we make are one of the strongest sources of meaning and purpose. They enrich our lives. After our death, they continue to have effects on the people we knew.

There are as many potential good and meaningful lives as there are people.

Thinking about what you would want for your own legacy can help you choose how best to live your life.

Think about your own legacy.

Will you leave memories that will give comfort, courage, or inspiration to those who have loved you? The memories that people have of you may influence them for the whole of their own lives and influence their approach to their life. Have you said all the things you want to say to them?

Are there physical objects that you want specific people to have after you're dead? These might be simple things – items that you know have meant something to others, or around which you have made memories together. What would those objects remind people of if they had them after you were gone? Parting gifts can have a deep and lasting meaning for those who receive them.

Are there people for whom you have special respon-
sibilities? Children, grandchildren, pupils, nephews,
nieces, or younger friends or colleagues? The
example you give them, perhaps even the particular beliefs and values you pass on to them, will be
a significant legacy, with ramifications you cannot
imagine now.

When those we love die, the traces of their lives
persist in myriad ways, from their descendants to
the deeds they have done, and in our memories of
them. We can still imagine speaking with them in
our own minds and – quite often – we know exactly
how they would have replied to us.

We carry their legacy forward in the human story
– just as the people coming after us will do when
we are gone.

We are all part of a long human story that continues after we are gone, just as it went on for hundreds of thousands of years before we were born.

This idea is very popular in readings at humanist funerals.

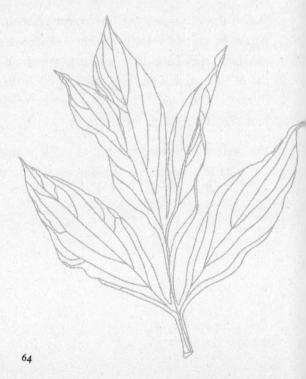

My favourite symbol is the tree of life. The human race is the trunk and branches of this tree, and individual men and women are the leaves, which appear one season, flourish for a summer, and then die. I am like a leaf of this tree, and one day I shall decay and fall, and become a pinch of compost about its roots.

But meanwhile I am conscious of the tree's flowing sap and steadfast strength. Deep down in my consciousness is the consciousness of a collective life, a life of which I am part, and to which I contribute a minute but unique extension.

When I die and fall, the tree remains, nourished to some small degree by my brief manifestation of life. Millions of leaves have preceded me and millions will follow me; the tree itself grows and endures.

Herbert Read

But I place one foot before the other, confident
   because
I know that everything we are right now is
   everything that was
That Watt Tyler, Woody Guthrie, Dostoevsky
   and Davy Jones
Have all dissolved into the ether and have crept
   into my bones
And all the cells in all the lines upon the backs
   of both my hands
Were once carved into the details of two feet
   upon the sand

Frank Turner

We are also all part of a wider human community through which we are all connected and this too is a popular idea in readings at humanist ceremonies.

> *No man is an island,*
> *Entire of itself,*
> *Every man is a piece of the continent,*
> *A part of the main.*
> *If a clod be washed away by the sea,*
> *Europe is the less.*
> *As well as if a promontory were.*
> *As well as if a manor of thy friend's*
> *Or of thine own were:*
> *Any man's death diminishes me,*
> *Because I am involved in mankind,*
> *And therefore never send to know for whom*
>   *the bell tolls;*
> *It tolls for thee.*

John Donne

Everything touches, life interweaves
Starlight and gunsmoke, ashes and leaves
Birdsong and thunder, acid and rain
Everything touches, unbroken chain

Chainsaw and rainbow, warrior and priest
Assassin off-duty, beauty and beast
Heartbeat and hightide, ebb and flow
Cardboard cathedral covered in snow

Snowdrop and gangrene, hangman and clown
Walls that divide us come tumbling down
Seen through the night the glimmer of day
Light is but darkness worn away

Past and future, distance and time
Atom to atom, water to wine
Look all around, what do you see?
Everything touches, you're touching me

Roger McGough

We have one life and it is short. The task of living is urgent.

When we think about what we will leave behind when we are gone, we get a better sense of what we should do and how we should live today.

When we think about what others have left behind in us – the memories, the influence, the impact – then we realise how important it is to live as fully as we can in our turn.

The meaning of life is to live it, as wholly as we can, as abundantly as we can, as bravely as we can, here and now, sharing the experience with others, caring for others as we care for ourselves, and accepting our responsibility for leaving the world better than we found it.

James Hemming

If you take Einstein's universe at face value — and there's no reason why you shouldn't, it's our best theory of space and time — then this picture of space-time, with events placed within it, suggests something wonderful, and I think quite magical. If I leave a place in space, then it doesn't cease to exist when I've left it, and in space-time, if I leave an event it doesn't cease to exist when I've left it.

So, that suggests that all those summers you spent with your mum and dad, or that first Christmas with your grandparents long ago, all those most precious memories of people and places, all those summers and winters past, and seasons yet to come, are out there. Somewhere in space time.

Brian Cox

The most important thing I learnt on Tralfamadore was that when a person dies he only appears to die. He is still very much alive in the past, so it is very silly for people to cry at his funeral. All moments, past, present, and future, always have existed, always will exist. The Tralfamadorians can look at all the different moments just the way we can look at a stretch of the Rocky Mountains, for instance.

They can see how permanent all the moments are, and they can look at any moment that interests them. It is an illusion we have here on Earth that one moment follows another one, like beads on a string, and that once a moment is gone it is gone forever. When any Tralfamadorian sees a corpse, all he thinks is that the dead person is in a bad condition in that particular moment, but that the same person is just fine in plenty of other moments.

Kurt Vonnegut

Back to nature

We'll be alive again in a thousand blades of grass, and a million leaves, we'll be falling in the raindrops and blowing in the fresh breeze, we'll be glittering in the dew under the stars and the moon, out there in the physical world, which is our true home and always was.

Philip Pullman

We humans are a part of nature, not separate from it. We're connected to every living thing on the planet.

When we die, our bodies decompose. They rot and return to the earth and are a source of nourishment for other living things if we are buried. If we are cremated or our bodies disposed of in other ways – even if our ashes are fired into space – we still return to nature, as every particle that made us goes on to form other things.

Humanist funeral ceremonies often contain reflections on this fact. The setting in which they are held may also reflect it, if bodies are buried in woodland or natural burial grounds, or ashes scattered in outdoors places.

Warm summer sun,
  Shine kindly here,
Warm southern wind,
  Blow softly here.
Green sod above,
  Lie light, lie light.
Good night, dear heart,
  Good night, good night.

Walt Whitman

Take me to some high place of heather,
     rock and ling,
Scatter my dust and ashes, feed me to
     the wind,
So that I will be part of all you see,
     the air you are breathing –
I'll be part of the curlew's cry and the
     soaring hawk,
The blue milkwort and the sundew hung
     with diamonds;
I'll be riding the gentle breeze as it blows
     through your hair,
Reminding you how we shared in the
     joy of living.

Ewan MacColl and Peggy Seeger

I know that nothing is destructible; things merely change forms. When the consciousness we know as life ceases, I know that I shall still be part and parcel of the world. I was a part before the sun rolled into shape and burst forth in the glory of change. I was, when the earth was hurled out from its fiery rim. I shall return with the earth to Father Sun, and still exist in substance when the sun has lost its fire, and disintegrated into infinity to perhaps become a part of the whirling rubble of space. Why fear? The stuff of my being is matter, ever changing, ever moving, but never lost.

Zora Neale Hurston

Portion of this yew
Is a man my grandsire knew,
Bosomed here at its foot:
This branch may be his wife,
A ruddy human life
Now turned to a green shoot.

These grasses must be made
Of her who often prayed,
Last century, for repose;
And the fair girl long ago
Whom I often tried to know
May be entering this rose.

So, they are not underground,
But as nerves and veins abound
In the growths of upper air,
And they feel the sun and rain,
And the energy again
That made them what they were!

Thomas Hardy

It can be comforting to focus sometimes on the fact that we really are aspects of the same physical system as everything else. We are each a bit of the universe—no more, no less. On the one hand that might sound cold and unfeeling; on the other hand it might sound new age, hippyish or naive. But it's factually true, and there is both calm and wonder to be found in the knowledge that everything that makes me up was around before me and will be around afterwards. These changes of state are part of the way of things. All the more wondrous, then, to have been able to experience this for a while. And perhaps a little less earth-shattering, then, that things change, swirl about, switch positions, and we become something else just as surely as other things became us.

Humanist celebrant Ewan Main

All the materials that we are made from were there at the beginning and they will be there at the end after we ourselves are gone. As we experience and understand the universe a little, we can also feel that we are part of it.

Now the land that I knew is a dream
And the line on the distance grows faint
So wide is my river
The horizon a sliver
The artist has run out of paint
Where the blue of the sea meets the sky
And the big yellow sun leads me home
I'm everywhere now
The way is a vow
To the wind of each breath by and by
The water sustains me without even trying
The water can't drown me, I'm done
With my dying

Johnny Flynn and Laura Marling

Our story is the story of the universe. Everything you love and everything you hate, of the thing you hold most precious, was assembled by the forces of nature in the first few minutes of the life of the universe, transformed in the hearts of the stars or created in their fiery deaths. And when you and I die, those pieces will be returned to the universe in the endless cycle of death and rebirth. What a wonderful thing it is to be part of that universe. What a story, what a majestic story.

Brian Cox

Saying goodbye to the physical remains of a loved one is a wrench. It can feel like a hook in the heart, an awful realisation that the person is really dead. It is reassuring to remember that when we die, we are completing the cycle that nature intended for us. Like leaves on a tree, we fall and are taken back to the very matter of the universe which is our eternal home.

Humanist celebrant Hester Brown

Living with grief

Death is the price of life.

George Orwell

Just as death is the price of life, the feeling of grief is the price of love.

Would you rather never feel grief but never have any love in your life? Few of us would.

We would rather love, even though this means we will inevitably experience loss and grief as a result.

I hold it true, whate'er befall;

I feel it when I sorrow most;

'Tis better to have loved and lost

Than never to have loved at all.

Alfred, Lord Tennyson

Consolation in the face of death can come from reflecting on all the ways in which the dead 'live on', but even for the most resilient and stoical person there is grief as well.

Grief is an inescapable part of the human experience. Intensity of grief is one measure of the importance of the time on this planet of those we have loved and it reflects the depth of the relationships we have with others. Without the darkness we cannot see the light.

This much I'm reasonably certain of —
that there are much worse emotions
to have to live with than sadness,
however vast and deep that sadness
might be. It can be uplifting,
invigorating, strengthening, motivating
and, above all, a powerful reminder
of how much that person still matters,
and always will.

Nelson Mandela

Think of those you care about, imagine them mourning when you die, and ask yourself how much sorrow you would wish them to bear. The answer would surely be: neither too much, nor for too long. You would wish them to come to terms with loss, and thereafter to remember the best of the past with joy, and you would wish them to continue life hopefully, which is the natural sentiment of the human condition.

If that is what we wish for those we will leave behind us when we die, then that is what we must believe would be desired by those who have already died. In that way we do justice to a conception of what their best and kindest wishes for us would be, and thereby, begin to restore the balance that is upset by this most poignant of life's sorrows.

A.C. Grayling

I do absolutely believe that this is it,
and I find huge comfort in that.
And anybody who knows us – John
and I – knows that we lived life to the
absolute full. We did not squeeze life
into the gaps between his treatment
because he died of cancer. He and
I both believed in people, and what
we can do, and what we achieve,
and what we give to each other.
That lasts. That absolutely lasts.

But I don't believe we're going to be reunited somewhere. And like I say, I'm happy with what we have, and what we had, and I don't need to be looking forward to anything else. It's absolutely terrible, it still is – daily, terrible . . . to be in a world without him. But the world with him was exceptionally lovely.

Janet Ellis, speaking after the death of her husband

In moments of great grief,
that's where you look and
immerse yourself. You realise
you are not immortal, you are
not a god, you are part of
the natural world and you
come to accept that.

David Attenborough,
following the death of his wife

You do come out of it, that's true. After a year, after five. But you don't come out of it like a train coming out of a tunnel, bursting through the Downs into sunshine and that swift, rattling descent to the Channel; you come out of it as a gull comes out of an oil-slick. You are tarred and feathered for life.

Julian Barnes

Your own funeral

Do not stand
    By my grave, and weep,
I am not there,
    I do not sleep.
I am a thousand winds that blow,
I am the diamond glints in snow,
I am the sunlight on ripened grain,
I am the gentle, autumn rain.
When you awaken with morning's hush
I am the swift upflinging rush
Of quiet birds in circling flight.
I am the day transcending night.
Do not stand
    at my grave and cry -
I am not there,
    I did not die.

Clare Harner

More and more people are choosing to meet with a humanist celebrant before they die, to start talking about and planning their own funeral. It's one of the ways that we can gain a sense of control over our own deaths and what follows. It also helps us to face up to death and come to terms with it.

By planning your own funeral, or part of it, you can also help the family and friends you leave behind face death more easily at what will be a difficult time for them.

I'd like the memory of me to be a
   happy one.
I'd like to leave an afterglow of smiles
   when life is done.
I'd like to leave an echo whispering
   softly down the ways,
Of happy times and laughing times
   and bright and sunny days.
I'd like the tears of those who grieve,
   to dry before the sun;
Of happy memories that I leave when
   life is done

Helen Lowrie Marshall

I was so lucky to be able to meet Jenny
myself last summer. She and Bob invited
me up to the bungalow in Whitehead
for a chat. It wasn't an easy conversation
because the subject was, well, today. What
Jenny wanted and what she didn't want
– from the music to the poetry to the
embarrassing stories about Bob when she
met him. You're in for a treat.

It was very clear to me that by asking me to come for a difficult talk, Jenny was not just being organised but she was doing it because she wanted to make things as easy as she possibly could for the people she cared about the most. And that in itself speaks volumes about her. And she was very clear that even though this is the most difficult time that many of you have ever experienced, she wanted today to be a celebration of her life. In Jenny's case there is a lot to talk about; it is no cliché or exaggeration to say that she fitted more into just sixty-five years than many of us would do given a hundred.

From a ceremony by humanist celebrant Stewart Holden

Having officiated at many funerals, I have witnessed the whole range of emotions exhibited by loved ones. Many feel overwhelmed by the responsibility of planning a 'perfect' funeral ceremony. For some, family dynamics add a further layer of emotion and, sometimes, unresolved conflict, to the already highly emotionally charged situation. Increasingly, I am asked to support individuals planning their own funeral – sometimes because of a life-limiting illness but not exclusively. Some may think planning your own funeral is about control but it is so very clearly not. At the end, control has no importance whatsoever, and, in actual fact, planning in advance is a very special gift to leave to a loved one.

The gift of knowing that they do not need to agonise over what should be or should not be; the gift that they will be doing exactly what you want; the gift that you loved them so very much that you spared them the pain of choosing coffins and music and readings and anything related to the event, rather than focusing on and grieving for their loved one. Everything planned will be lovely, but all they wanted was to think about you and not worry that they may choose an inappropriate word, the wrong something or other. When you plan for yourself, they can just be with their memories of you . . . perfect; your final, loving gift.

Humanist celebrant Susan Dobinson

'I am convinced more people plan their own funerals than we ever know about. Those little games between friends of 'What music would you play?' that happen over a few glasses of wine, or 'What kind of funeral would you want?' are often based on the real wish to have a life reflected accurately, and yet few summon the courage to commit those wishes to paper and share them with those who matter. It is such a shame, because it is an opportunity to gift those you love with a template for a funeral which they can deliver knowing you would have approved. And that can be a precious gift at a difficult time.

Families can be wary of their loved one actively discussing their funeral – perhaps fearful that acknowledgement of death is 'giving up' or 'ceasing the fight'. It isn't. For many it is an empowering experience at a time of rapidly decreasing choices. Choosing the music, choosing reading or poetry and recalling the moments of your life that matter most to you – this is an opportunity to take control of your life's narrative when people are sticking needles in you and feeding you pills. Far from 'giving up', I would argue that it is an act of defiance in the face of death and a thoughtful gift to loved ones.'

Humanist celebrant Jo Beddington

To say that Neal was honest with death would be bordering on understatement, and whilst we gather here today with the firm intention of celebrating Neal's life, I hope you'll understand if I begin by talking about Neal's death, and more specifically his attitude towards it.

Neal phoned me for the first time in November and said he'd like to have a chat. In the end I was fortunate to meet him and his family four times over the past few months, as we worked together to ensure that every part of today's proceedings was exactly what Neal wanted.

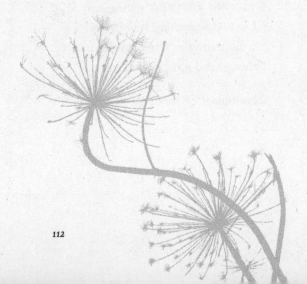

When we first met at his home, Neal explained in a remarkably matter-of-fact way that he had been diagnosed with terminal cancer and given nine to twelve months to live. That diagnosis had been given more than three years ago, meaning that Neal found himself in the conflicted position of being understandably devastated at his misfortune and yet also grateful for having had so much longer than he'd expected with his beloved wife, his daughter and his step-daughters. It is rare that even those who are terminally ill have the strength of character to even discuss plans for celebrating their life, but Neal's motivation didn't come from ego or pride but simply the desire to make things easier for his own family when this time came.

From a ceremony by humanist celebrant Stewart Holden

HUMANIST
FUNERALS

This should be not a tomb ritual but a harvest ritual – the bringing in of a life.

Harold Blackham

A humanist ceremony can be held in any place and it can be any length. It may last half an hour or be open-ended.

It may take place in a crematorium or burial ground, in a village hall or community centre, in the open air, inside your home – anywhere.

The ceremony may take place with the coffin present, or the body in a shroud, or with an urn containing ashes, or in the absence of any physical remains.

It may take place in the weeks following a death or it may take place months afterwards and be more like a memorial meeting.

It may be a single event – a burial, a cremation, or a party with everyone invited. Or it may take place in stages: perhaps a private cremation first, an ashes-centred funeral ceremony some time later, and a further scattering of ashes some time after that. Or it could involve a ceremony with friends and family followed by a private burial for close family only.

The funeral that takes place close to someone's death is only the beginning of the process and rituals of saying goodbye, coping with grief, and accepting loss.

Wherever and whenever it is held, a funeral is one of the first steps we take in making sense of our loss and beginning to live without the presence of the person we have lost.

Almost always, the funeral involves a gathering together of friends and family to eat and drink and share memories. But it begins with a ceremony, intended to give structure, meaning, and sense to what we are going through.

Humanist celebrants are trained experts in making sure that the ceremony does just this.

Unique circumstances

Although a humanist funeral is about honouring and commemorating *the life* of a person, the reason it is happening is because that person has died. So, a ceremony will often start with the circumstances of the death.

Just as every person is unique, every death is different, and we feel differently about each one. Our feelings depend on our relationship to the person who has died and the circumstances of their death.

A funeral has many purposes: to honour the unique life of the person who has died, to offer comfort to those who knew them, to bring a community together, to begin healing, create a space for the sharing of memories, offer a definitive punctuation mark in the experience of bereavement, or simply to formally say goodbye.

The circumstances surrounding a death will influence the tone of a humanist funeral ceremony.

Sometimes a bereavement is entirely
unexpected, but often it is long predicted
and, to whatever extent is possible,
prepared for. Or, at least, not unsurprising.
In those situations, we exchange
comforting truths with one another, and
we silently rehearse them to ourselves:

'It was at the end of a long illness'

'They had a good innings'

'We all knew it was coming'

'It was probably for the best, in the end'

But the truth is: it's always a shock.
It's always unexpected. No matter
how certainly we know the moment is
approaching – no matter how totally
predictable, run-of-the-mill or natural part
of us knows that moment is – emotionally
and physically, it's always a shock. How
could it not be? How, really, could
anyone properly prepare themselves to
comprehend the loss of another?

Certainly, some situations are more traumatic than others, or traumatic in different ways. People's experiences aren't the same, and they aren't necessarily equal. But no matter how 'simple' or 'normal' or 'expected' a death is, those left behind – including ourselves – need all the kindness, patience and tolerance we can muster. Because no matter what any of us says to each other, it is definitely a shock.

Humanist celebrant Ewan Main

This is unimaginable in terms of your own shock and blind grief, but we must take some consolation that Peter wouldn't have known what happened. There are no good ways to shuffle off this mortal coil, but quickly and as painlessly as possible is up there with what we would all probably want.

But we are left behind, shocked and stunned.

I took comfort in this quote to help guide us through the next part of this ceremony. Oscar Wilde wrote, 'Laughter is not at all a bad beginning for a friendship, and it is by far the best ending for one.' And Peter came into my life accompanied by so much bloody laughter. Let us all take turns in sharing some of those stories.

From a ceremony by humanist celebrant
Zena Birch

Listen. There is this silence now. This stillness.
Gradually we will get used to it. But, for now,
It is strange. You have left such a gap.
Our world is in shock, holding its breath
But listen closer – all your laughter, all your love
is still ringing out. Still holding us.
All our memories of you are still with us.
All the love we shared is still in every one of us.
And although we ache from this loss of you,
you will always be here – as still and steady,
and fierce, as any star.
Look. You are shining
bright through all our skies.
We thank you
for sharing your life with us.

Char March

Many people die in old age at the end of a long life:

Occurring while she slept, she would not have known that death had furtively arrived and embraced her. To us, her passing was sudden and unexpected. Even so, it was ever so peaceful, mercifully painless and, for her, the perfect way to 'bow out' of life.

We may feel glad for Nell's sake that she died where, when and how she did. She had always hoped that she would end her days at the farm rather than inexorably waste away in a hospice, nursing or residential home. She had absolutely no desire to live as long as her mother who passed away at the grand and venerable old age of ninety-eight. Moreover, a woman who had lived a fulfilling life in the magnificent outdoors of the countryside, she could not face the prospect of suffering the demoralisation, incapacitation and indignity of a debilitating and protracted illness. We may feel glad, therefore, that her wishes, on all three counts, were granted.

From a ceremony by humanist celebrant
Gary Vaudin

An individual human existence should be like a river – small at first, narrowly contained within its banks, and rushing passionately past boulders and over waterfalls. Gradually the river grows wider, the banks recede, the waters flow more quietly, and – in the end – without any visible break, they become merged in the sea, and painlessly lose their individual being. The man or woman who in old age can see his or her life in this way, will not suffer from the fear of death, since the things they care for will continue.

Bertrand Russell

We often think of death as a cruel enemy, taking away those we love, but for those who are suffering or have reached the end of their endurance, it can come as a quiet friend, closing the curtains, blowing out the light, and settling us into a last sleep, free from pain and weariness.

From a ceremony by humanist celebrant Felicity Harvest

Why do I think of Death
As a friend?
It is because he is a scatterer,
He scatters the human frame
The nerviness and the great pain,
Throws it on the fresh fresh air
And now it is nowhere
Only sweet Death does this,
Sweet Death, Kind Death,
Of all the gods you are the best.

Stevie Smith

Now that I am wearied of the day,

my ardent desire shall happily receive

the starry night

like a sleepy child.

Hands, stop all your work.

Brow, forget all your thinking.

All my senses now

yearn to sink into slumber.

Hermann Hesse

At every turning of my life
I came across
Good friends,
Friends who stood by me
Even when time raced me by.
Farewell, farewell
My friends
I smile and
Bid you goodbye.
No, shed no tears
For I need them not
All I need is your smile.
If you feel sad
Do think of me
For that's what I'd like.
When you live in the hearts
Of those you love
Remember then
You never die.

Rabindranath Tagore

Diagnosed with Parkinson's disease around ten years ago, Tom was astute enough to know that he faced the prospect of an inexorably progressive and protracted decline in his health. A man with a remarkable tenacity for life, however, he did not allow this devastating diagnosis to overwhelm him psychologically. Placing faith and trust in the expertise of medical professionals, he knew that, with modern drug treatments, he could expect to obtain considerable relief from his illness and continue to lead a life of reasonably good quality. Even so, 'the writing was on the wall': as time passed and his health deteriorated further, there came a point when he realised that the inevitable was nigh and, while he was still fully *compos mentis*, meticulously prepared for this day. The calm, dignified, down-to-earth and pragmatic manner with which he countenanced death was characteristic of the man he was. Such traits, however, were also characteristic of the way he chose to live.

From a ceremony by humanist celebrant Gary Vaudin

In nature, cessation of function, followed by transformation of the physical elements is part of life's continuity. It is a commonplace, but an important one, that death and decay are the servants of life. Fallen leaves change into the humus on which next year's seedlings feed: so the death and transformation of autumn is essential to spring. Death is, therefore, a condition of life and constitutes half its rhythm. Death does not end life but is part of it, one of nature's transformations, as we work our way through its cycles.

A.C. Grayling

The death of a child

It is particularly difficult to accept the death of
a child, which is so far from the 'order of things'
which we expect. Death does not belong at the
beginning of life. Our children are expected to
live beyond our own years, and when the cycle
of life is broken, it has an enormous impact on
the community of family and friends of which
a baby is undeniably a part, both in anticipation
of their arrival, and in the time, however long or
short, that they spend with a family. Grief and
love go hand in hand – allowing yourselves to
love someone, even for such a short time, lets
them know just how much they were loved,
and how they will be remembered.

There is little which can possibly be said to give any consolation, or to help to explain or give meaning to what happened to a child who has died. What we can do as celebrants is to celebrate their life, acknowledge the pain which accompanies this loss, and provide a way to help a bereaved family commit their child into their hearts and memories.

Humanist celebrant Kate Owens-Palmer

We cannot, after all, judge
a biography by its length,
by the number of pages in it;
we must judge by the richness
of the contents . . . sometimes
the 'unfinisheds' are among the
most beautiful symphonies.

Viktor E Frankl

His laughter was better than birds in the
   morning, his smile
Turned the edge of the wind, his memory
Disarms death and charms the surly grave.
Early he went to bed, too early we
Saw his light put out; yet we could not grieve
More than a little while,
For he lives in the earth around us, laughs
   from the sky.

Cecil Day Lewis

This was a life that had hardly begun

No time to find your place in the sun

No time to do all you could have done

But we loved you enough for a lifetime

No time to enjoy the world and its wealth

No time to take life down off the shelf

No time to sing the songs of yourself

Though you had enough love for a lifetime

Those who live long endure sadness and tears

But you'll never suffer the sorrowing years

No betrayal, no anger, no hatred, no fears

Just love – only love – in your lifetime.

Mary Yarnall

Some parents choose to have a funeral for a child that is stillborn or for a miscarriage

I think it is important when considering the funeral of a child in this context to acknowledge the life that had been hoped for and in almost all instances, the name the parents have given their child. The funeral ceremony can be an opportunity to talk about how and why that name was chosen, honour it, and give context. We shouldn't be frightened to talk about the hopes and dreams that had existed from the moment they knew of their child's conception. Talking and sharing these thoughts are part of the necessary healing process – which a funeral in this instance is so good for.

Humanist celebrant Zena Birch

I don't think most people truly understand
how much is lost when a baby dies. You
don't just lose a baby, you also lose the
1 and 2 and 10 and 16 year old she would
have become. You lose Christmas mornings,
loose teeth, first days of school . . . you
just lost it all.

Stephanie Page Cole

My friend Pip lost her third baby before he was born. She knew that her baby was dead before she gave birth to him. Pip and her husband hadn't thought about what they were going to do afterwards. But then when they were asked, they realised that what they wanted to do was bring him home. It wasn't a funeral, she said – it was a homecoming. They buried him in their garden, in the orchard. Their other two children helped to bury him and plant a tree on his grave.

An echo of an ancient practice. The baby was part of the family, part of the family tapestry. And he is not forgotten.

Alice Roberts

I adapted this for a young couple mourning the loss of their pre-term baby in very distressing circumstances. It comes from a poem, 'Four Candles for You', and can be adapted to suit any circumstances but is great for a very small gathering, accompanied by a candle-lighting ritual.

Humanist celebrant Natalie Charles

Four Candles for Our Baby

The first candle represents our memories.
We will never forget the love and happiness you brought.
This second candle we light is our grief.
The pain of our loss is intense.
It reminds us of how hard it is to let you go.
The third candle is for the courage we need
To confront our sorrow, to heal around it
And to comfort each other.
What we have been through will make us stronger still.

This fourth candle we light for our hope.
Through us your light will continue to shine,
And will guide us towards a happier future.
We will never forget you.

We Were Parents

You played hide and seek
through our dreams for years
before you arrived.

Then, once we'd tigged you
– that squirm of blur
inside that pulsing screen –

we lay at night trying
not to giggle; straining
to hear your heartbeat.

You made us laugh a lot,
and disagree, and talk till 3am
of names, and whose nose you'd get.

And then you, who had lived
with us such a blink of time,
left.

And we are left, holding
onto nothing but naming books,
and our lurching world.

For you braced your whole
13cm self, and threw our
planet off its axis.

Char March

Not everyone dies of natural causes, some deaths are violent. And in some cases, people take their own lives.

We cannot know what is in the mind of someone who takes their own life, what their thoughts are and how they concluded that it was not possible for them to go on. There can be no real understanding of the depression and insecurity that they must have felt. It will have taken courage to take that ultimate step, and, to them, a peaceful and sudden death seemed preferable to living on with a tormented mind and an uncertain future. No-one who knows the circumstances of the death will remain untouched by it or fail to ask themselves what they could have done to prevent it.

In the funeral ceremony the celebrant should ask for people to respect the fact that their loved one had the right to make this decision. That they should be gentle in their judgement of that decision. The second essential element of the celebration is that the deceased be forgiven for the decision that they made. It will be necessary to make a real effort to do this. Anger must be put aside as must any feeling of being betrayed or abandoned. Without this forgiveness there can be no closure. Finally, and this will usually be towards the end of the ceremony, everyone present must be told to forgive themselves. They must forgive themselves and stop feeling guilty. If the celebrant can effectively communicate these elements, as well as all the other components of a humanist funeral, they will help the bereaved to come to closure.

Humanist celebrant Graeme Ward

Sadly over the years, I've been asked to take the funerals of many people who have ended their own lives, and these funerals, by their very nature, are so often extremely sensitive; particularly in terms of making fitting word choices and creating the right atmosphere. Working very closely with the next of kin is essential in ensuring the tone and content is as comfortable as it can possibly be for them, and that the person is honoured in the best way. But guidance is regularly needed by bereaved families who find themselves in this dreadful situation and therefore, the relationship they build with their celebrant, in the lead up to the funeral day, is key.

Whereas many families, in my experience, do not want the nature of the death spoken about, some feel it is essential to make mention of the choice the person took, not avoiding 'the elephant in the room'. Active listening and gentle questioning is needed as the funeral ceremony is prepared, so that this issue is handled well.

Humanist celebrant Jane Blackman

When you go out into the woods and you look at trees, you see all these different trees. And some of them are bent, and some of them are straight, and some of them are evergreens, and some of them are whatever. And you look at the tree and you allow it. You see why it is the way it is. You sort of understand that it didn't get enough light, and so it turned that way. And you don't get all emotional about it. You just allow it. You appreciate the tree. The minute you get near humans, you lose all that. And you are constantly saying, 'you are too that', or 'I'm too this' . . . And so I practice turning people into trees. Which means appreciating them just the way they are.

Richard Alpert

Different relationships

I've often thought an important part of
a funeral ceremony is that it can make
people reappraise their own lives and
what really matters to them.

Humanist celebrant Michael Ashbridge

Not every death is the same to us because our relationship with each person is different.

Relationships can be easy or complex, strained, chaotic, intimate or distant. We don't need to pretend anything in a humanist ceremony. Humanists understand the complexity of human relationships, so humanist celebrants are trained to accept the full spectrum of characters and scenarios.

This may have been the person who you loved most in the whole world, or perhaps they were so difficult you spent far more time avoiding them than anything else. Humanist celebrants are experienced in responding to all sorts of people and relationships.

Parents

Parents come in all sorts and types but
there's a sense in which they remain
anchors in life and losing them can be
so sad, particularly when the relationship
has been less than ideal. People may
say they didn't get on with their mum
or dad and also that there's a great deal
they taught them – a great deal they'll
miss, too. When family relationships
are seriously troubled or broken, there
is often a much harder grieving process,
but the funeral can be a time to reflect
and even to heal.

Humanist celebrant Sue Baumbach

Our parents cast long shadows over our lives. When we grow up we imagine that we can walk into the sun, free of them. We don't realise until it's too late that we have no choice in the matter, they're always ahead of us. We carry them within us all our lives, in the shape of our faces, the way we walk, the sound of our voice, our skin, our hair, our hands, our heart. We try all our lives to separate ourselves from them and only when they are dead do we find we are indivisible.

We grow to expect that our parents, like the weather, will always be with us. Then they go, leaving a mark like a handprint on glass or a soft kiss on a rainy day, and with their deaths we are no longer children.

Richard Eyre

As we look back over time

We find ourselves wondering . . .

Did we remember to thank you enough

For all you have done for us?

For all the times you were by our sides

To help and support us . . .

To celebrate our successes

To understand our problems

And accept our defeats?

Or for teaching us by your example,

The value of hard work, good judgement,

Courage and integrity?

We wonder if we ever thanked you

For the sacrifices you made.

To let us have the very best?

And for the simple things

Like laughter, smiles and times we shared?

If we have forgotten to show our

Gratitude enough for all the things you did,

We're thanking you now.

And we are hoping you knew all along,

How much you meant to us.

Clare Jones

Spouse, partner, or lover

It's so curious: one can resist tears and
'behave' very well in the hardest hours
of grief. But then someone makes you a
friendly sign behind a window, or one
notices that a flower that was in bud
only yesterday has suddenly blossomed,
or a letter slips from a drawer . . . and
everything collapses.

Collette

Do not miss me, because I will always be with you.

In every drop of rain that touches your tongue, in every breath of air you inhale.

In the tips of the leaves that you brush with your fingertips as you pass by.

I will be there, in every moment. I am not gone, I am only altered, from this state of matter to another.

For a moment, for too brief a moment, I was the one that loved you, but now that I am changed, I am the air, the moon, the stars.

For we are all made of stars, my beloved.

So do not miss me, because I do not die; I transform – into the wind in the tops of the trees, the wave on the ocean, the pebbles under your foot, the dust on your bookshelves, the midnight sky.

Rowan Coleman

A child

There is a Korean proverb that says:
'When a parent dies, they are buried
in the ground. When a child dies they
are buried in the parent's heart.' When
I look at the faces of parents who have
lost a child, it is clear they have buried
that child not just in their heart, but in
their lips, eyes and skin, too.

Humanist celebrant Jenny Bullough

I was only eleven when my brother died, he was eight. He was killed in a traffic accident. I knew even at a young age that being told he had gone to a better place didn't salve any of the pain, the hurt or the confusion. He hadn't been sick and he wasn't old. His death shattered everything. One of the things which did help was seeing him: my mum brought him back from a cold and dark funeral directors to lay at rest in our front room. I also had a few people close to me who told me the truth rather than trying to protect me with platitudes. I truly recommend this. Young minds can handle the truth and can see through lies, no matter how kindly. I'm pretty certain, in small steps as time went by, that this is in part what led me to being a funeral celebrant. Nothing can make the funeral ceremony of a child feel OK, it is true that it feels against the natural order of things, but equally, few things are more important than getting this ceremony right. I am so grateful for the training my humanist funeral celebrant colleagues and I get, so we can support people through this, the toughest of times.

Humanist celebrant Zena Birch

Friends

People may forget

what you said,

people may forget

what you did.

But they will never

forget how you

made them feel.

Attributed to Maya Angelou

And what am I supposed to do with all the
love I had for her? Surely it's not healthy
to have a surplus. Could I monetise it, like
everything else these days? Frankly, I'd prefer
to squander it as recklessly as possible.
Or perhaps I should spread it around, and
try to redress at least one of the inequalities
she despised so much. But love has no
economy, and every day it swells inside me,
a fresh supply with no demand to satisfy it.
I'll need to find new customers eventually,
otherwise my heart will grow grotesquely
heavy, and burst from its confinement,
and I'll have to carry it around with me in
a wheelbarrow.

Paul Barratt Davies

Life is like a grand circle dance: we step into the circle when we are born and those already dancing stretch out a hand to us and teach us the steps. We, as we grow, reach out to new dancers and draw them into the circle. Some of us are really nifty dancers and some, perhaps, clumsy, but all have something to take and all have something to give. A few light up the dance with their skill, others simply keep the circle going. Some dance for many years, some only days, and all of us, as our time comes to its end, step out of the circle – and the dance goes on.

Humanist celebrant Maggie Platts

Pets

For many people a pet is not just an animal but a much-loved member of the family, sharing in our joys and pleasures and giving companionship.

Pets help provide structure to the days of their human companions, they give meaning and purpose to many lives. The death of pets is also often a child's first experience of death and some type of ceremony can help to teach valuable lessons about loss and life.

All I need to know about life I learned from my dog

Never pass up the opportunity to go for a joy ride.

Allow the experience of fresh air and the wind in your face to be pure ecstasy.

When loved ones come home, always run to greet them.

Run, romp, and play daily.

Be loyal.

Never pretend to be something you're not.

Eat with gusto and enthusiasm.

If what you want lies buried, dig until you find it.

When someone is having a bad day, be silent, sit close by and nuzzle them gently.

Thrive on affection and let people touch you – enjoy back rubs and pats on your neck.

When you leave your yard, make it an adventure.

Avoid biting when a simple growl will do.

No matter how often you're scolded, don't pout
– run right back and make friends.

Bond with your pack.

On cold nights, curl up in front of a crackling fire.

When you're excited, speak up.

When you're happy, dance around and wag your
entire body.

Delight in the simple joy of a long walk.

If you stare at someone long enough, eventually
you'll get what you want.

Don't go out without ID.

Leave room in your schedule for a good nap.

Always give people a friendly greeting.

If it's not wet and sloppy, it's not a real kiss.

Anonymous

You told me that when Sam was dying you would tell him all the time how grateful you were for everything he had done for you both, and how thankful you were to him for all the joy he had brought to your lives. There is no kinder nor more generous act of love than to ease him from pain. He was loved, cared for, spoiled, enjoyed, played with, and an inextricable part of your family and will forever remain so. Goodbye Sam.

From a ceremony for a pet by humanist celebrant Zena Birch

Making it personal

It is easy to think that a funeral should be a sombre or a wholly sad occasion, but is this what the person who has died would have wanted? If it is, then it's a fine choice. But a ceremony full of colour and the celebration of a life is just as correct if that is what is appropriate.

Put the person at the centre of the ceremony and everything else will fall into place.

What is wonderful about humanist
funerals is that they are collaborations
between family (for family read friends
too) and the celebrant. The celebrant
brings their expertise to make the
process of creating a ceremony easier
for the family, but it is the family who
set the tone and decide the content. And
usually the family finds it a therapeutic
and empowering experience. When a
funeral has gone well the family says
to me, 'You helped make that a positive
experience. I thought it was going to
be awful but actually I now have good
memories to take away'.

Humanist celebrant Hester Brown

'It's how he would have wanted to be remembered!'

Wonderful words to hear after conducting a funeral, and often heard where there had been laughter in a ceremony. Some might wonder if it is appropriate to laugh at such a time, in the crematorium or burial ground, where people are saying their final formal farewell, but I would argue that, because all lives have joy as well as sadness in them, it's vital to bring some of that into a celebration of life. It's OK to share the jokes which the deceased might have told, even if they might be on the risqué side – remember them as they truly were, and express some of their personality there.

A humanist funeral isn't about sugar-coating a person's life. It's about celebrating them, warts and all, and if they were funny, or rude, or a practical joker, bring those elements into their ceremony. Talk about the hilarious antics they got up to, and the stories they told about things they had done which made people laugh helplessly when they were still alive. Make it real.

Laughter is cathartic in the same way as tears are, and both are perfectly appropriate at a funeral or memorial ceremony. And I hope, as people exit a chapel afterwards, to hear:

'She would have loved that!'

Humanist celebrant Kate Owens-Palmer

The most appropriate thing in a humanist funeral is that you celebrate your loved one the way they would have wanted. If that means we're all going to attend wearing pink tutus, or that we're going to play 'Anarchy in the UK', then that's fine. Tell your celebrant what you want from the service and they will work their hardest to deliver that for you. Everyone from your celebrant to your funeral director will have a network of contacts and ideas, so talk through your thoughts with them. There is a whole array of personalisation options for ceremonies nowadays, from individual hearses to customised coffins, from live music performance to conducting all or part of the ceremony yourself.

Humanist celebrant Adele Chaplin

The dead are not silent at a humanist funeral. They are present in every recollection shared, song chosen and even in reflection, where personal memories are silently revisited. Their body is in the coffin, but their essence – what they mean to those they met and how they influenced them, is celebrated.

A good and honest funeral will have mourners leaving with the thought, 'They would have liked that.'

Humanist celebrant Jo Beddington

A funeral started me on my journey to become a celebrant. My father's death in 2009 was my first 'big' bereavement and my first experience of the tidal wave of grief. My brother and I had no experience of organising a funeral – most people don't – but we knew as dad was an atheist it wouldn't be a church service. I had hoped to stand up and say something at the ceremony but realised a few days before that I simply wasn't going to be able to. Instead my brother spoke and my cousin and dad's brother all contributed stories and memories. It was a standard 30-minute 'slot' at the crematorium but it felt like we got close to giving dad a fitting send-off. Everyone walked out of the chapel to the strains of a song by The Goons which put a smile on everyone's face. He would have loved that.

And after weeks of riding the grief rollercoaster I felt lighter after the ceremony – I could think of dad as the person he had been rather than the really sick old man he had become in his last years. How powerful is that?! We had somehow managed to celebrate our kind and loving father. When I signed up to train as a funeral celebrant I was surprised at how fascinating I found the whole subject of death and how we think about funerals and celebrating a life. I don't find being involved in the death industry to be especially morbid. It gives me tremendous satisfaction to know that I have helped a family to capture the essence of someone and to help them celebrate their loved one.

Humanist celebrant Sue Walder

The words contained within a humanist funeral ceremony are particularly important. As we are not offering platitudes of eternal life or relying upon scripture designed to offer comfort based on or around a god or deity, a scripted, formulaic template fails to hit the spot. A humanist funeral ceremony script is packed to the brim with words that will sound familiar to you, full of relevant information about the life of the person who has died, filled with story and anecdote. I have often found that the creation of the script itself is a really useful tool in the grieving process of those involved; the reflection and reminiscence required and the process of talking about the person is helpful in so many ways.

Humanist celebrant Zena Birch

Give sorrow words. The grief

that does not speak

Whispers the o'erfraught heart,

and bids it break.

William Shakespeare

The magnificent Vicky Peck had four ceremonies. The first was her immediate ceremony at the crematorium, this was mid Covid-19 restrictions so only twelve people were allowed to be there. This was intimate, full of raw grief and filled with words she herself had spoken to me from her hospice so that her husband wouldn't have to try to find words amidst his grief. He knew she needed more. So a year later we created three ceremonies for one weekend: one, intimate again and personal for the interment of her ashes at the cemetery with a few more of the people who should have been there but Covid denied. The second was a memorial service in a cricket club for all of her friends and colleagues, still desperate to be able to honour her life. This began with many stories collected by me from friends over the year to make the room feel like a safe space to share and concluded with an open floor: anyone who wanted to shared a story whilst holding a tea timer – an anecdote the length of time it takes to brew the perfect cup of tea. As a former employee of Yorkshire Tea, this would have tickled her pink. And then finally a small contextualising ceremony preceding a live concert – made up of her favourite bands in her favourite gig venue – with all proceeds raising money for the cancer charities and hospice she had allocated before she died. Each honoured her life in a different way and was in keeping for all the different groups of people who knew and loved her. What a legacy. May everyone who wishes to have such things be able to! Humanist celebrants are here to make sure this can happen.

Humanist celebrant Zena Birch

Practices: old and new

Although every humanist funeral is unique, some elements are almost always present: reflections on life and death, the story of the life of the person who has died, music, readings of poetry or prose, and tributes from friends and family.

Beyond this, there are a number of actions or rituals that might be included, either traditional or modern and bespoke. These will be completely tailored to the specific circumstances of the ceremony.

There is really no limit to what **contemporary rituals** can be created. They often evolve from the work a celebrant will do with the bereaved and reflect the life and interests of the person. Symbolic gestures may help to illuminate something words cannot, or provide ways of discovering how to give meaning to our loss through action.

The important thing is that the action says something authentic about the person who has died and brings comfort or meaning to those present. As well as meaning something about the person who has died, they help to bring people together as a collective at a time when we can feel isolated in grief. They can give a physical embodiment of the connectedness of family and friends.

Why do we find it important to honour the wishes of people who have died? In the days and weeks surrounding their death; in planning the funeral; in the years ahead; as we live our lives? Particularly if we don't believe in an afterlife, what's the point when it will make no difference to them either way?

I think, deep down, it's because we believe we only have one life. The very fact that we will reach the end of ours makes it all the more urgent to do something worthwhile, leave something tangible, have an effect on others, improve something, make a difference – no matter how small. The ultimate aim, as we gradually move in the direction of the finishing point, is for it to have somehow made a difference that we existed. That's it: our prime directive, and a fundamental part of the definition of being human.

It's important to behave, when we can, in accordance with our values. It's important to remind ourselves, and affirm with one another, that these are our values. And 'it must matter that each person existed' is a core value – perhaps the core value. It's what gets us through the day, inspires and guides us.

We honour the wishes, ideas and examples of those who have died, then, not in the hope that they will do the same for us. That's a transaction that is strictly non-reciprocal. It's less calculated, and less conscious, than that. We do it because it's an expression of our deeply held humanity.

Humanist celebrant Ewan Main

Eulogies are reflections on the person who has died by those who knew and loved them, which are spoken by those people themselves, rather than being read by the celebrant. Anecdotes and reflections on the character and influence of the person can have great poignancy and meaning when delivered by those who knew them personally and grieve for them.

'I've often encouraged family and friends to read each other's tributes rather than their own: a grandmother reading her grandson's words, for example, and vice-versa. It tends to be much easier emotionally for the readers.'

Humanist celebrant Sara Scott

Music can be used in many different ways in ceremonies. Almost always there will be music for when the coffin or ashes are brought into the place where the ceremony is being held and different music for when either the coffin or ashes depart or the people attending leave.

At longer ceremonies, there may be music within the ceremony as well as before and after. This provides an opportunity for contemplation and reflection for those present to think about their own memories of the person who has died.

Music is most often recorded, but can also be live. Funerals may have choirs, bands, or solo singers or musicians.

The choice of music is entirely shaped by the life and character of the person whose funeral it is, but often they will also be pieces that mean something to those present.

We're now going to perform an act of remembrance for Charlie. And this is where the stones come in.

Part of Jewish traditional bereavement practice is to place small visitation stones on graves to respect and remember the deceased. Interestingly, the Hebrew word for pebble is "tz'ror" but the word also means "bond".

So, by placing your stone or pebble by the tree you will be symbolising the loving bonds that connect you all to Charlie.

It is customary to place the stone with the left hand, so can I ask you all now to follow the family by placing your stone or pebble under Charlie's cherry tree.'

From a funeral ceremony by humanist celebrant Sue Walder

Pictures are a relatively new addition to funerals in the UK but some funerals now will have a framed picture of the person next to the coffin or urn.

Many crematoria now have video screens where slideshows of photographs can be played before the ceremony begins, during a period of reflection during the ceremony, or as part of the ceremony.

Images can be powerful triggers of happy memories for those present and they can also convey a lot of the personality of the person whose funeral it is.

In places where there is drink or food after a cere-mony, or when funerals or memorials are held in places like village halls or community centres, a **memory table** may feature.

The table may hold pictures of the person but also photos of places that were important to them or of people from their life. Also included might be items like a favourite book or item of clothing – anything that will remind people of their personality or approach to life.

As a way of involving different people, they can be invited to bring their own object for the table and to speak to others about what it means to them.

Candles can play an effective part in ceremonies with great symbolism, but different uses will seem more or less appropriate to different people.

Candles can be lit in the ceremony and left burning as those present depart:

'We light these candles as a symbol of the warmth and light that she brought to our lives, and when we leave this place we leave them burning, just as the light of her life continues to be an inspiration for us.'

Alternatively, they may be extinguished:

'I invite each of you to come forward and, with affection, love, reverence and tenderness, put out a candle, symbolising your ultimate parting from him.'

Flowers and trees can have many uses in humanist funerals. Cut flowers have an ancient symbolic association with the end of a life and both flowers and trees are reminders of the cycle of nature of which human death is a part.

Placing flowers on the coffin as you depart has become increasingly popular:

'Now as we leave this place having said farewell together, you can each lay a flower on the coffin and, if you wish, take a moment to say your own private goodbye to her.'

Flowers or flower petals can also be thrown by family and friends into a grave as a symbolic alternative to earth.

Planting a tree as part of a memorial ceremony or giving seeds to guests for them to plant in memory of the person both allow nature itself to be a memorial to a person.

In some countries it is possible for a body to be composted rather than buried or reduced to ashes, with relatives receiving the composted remains for their gardens.

As part of the tribute for a radio superintendent I said 'David travelled all over the world. He worked on many different ships and met many different people. As usual, he rarely talked about his experiences, which are thought to have involved a lot of time in the Far East, including having tea with geishas. One story he did tell was about being held at gunpoint on the ship when they were docked in Basra. He did not seem particularly fazed by this experience, commenting that it was bandits who 'just wanted money'. He said he would leave the family a message in Morse code, but they haven't found it yet.'

At the committal, I then said: 'As David didn't leave that Morse code message for you, here's one from you to him', and one of his sons came forward and played a message to David in Morse code on his phone.

Humanist celebrant Felicity Harvest

Clive had been a keen actor all his life, involved from a young age in amateur dramatic groups and often going to the theatre. In adulthood, he became a drama teacher. When his husband, family and I were planning his funeral after his sudden and unexpected death, we talked about which symbolic gesture would best represent someone who was such fun and so full of life and love for all his many friends. It had to be a collective experience, inclusive and from the heart. We decided to give him a one-minute standing ovation.

After the words of farewell, I announced what we were going to do and asked everyone present – almost 200 people – to stand. There followed sixty seconds of the loudest applause and cheers you have ever heard – the rafters were shaken! It was the most moving thing: a real physical release for everyone still in deep shock, like a roar, with smiles and whoops, mingled with tears too. It was the perfect way to share our appreciation of him. And he would have loved it.

Humanist celebrant Deborah Hooper

At the funeral of a croupier, I ended with the words:

'In a moment, we will hear the theme tune to one of her very favourite TV programmes, which was, unsurprisingly, Ab Fab. After that, at my signal, we will wind up this part of the day in a way which Sue would certainly have appreciated, with a very special five gun salute. Take care of yourselves, and of each other.'

Five waiters then popped open bottles of fizz.

Humanist celebrant Felicity Harvest

I went to the ceremony of one grandfather who had infamously allowed his very many children and grandchildren to draw with felt tips all over the house when they were little (to the displeasure of grandma). Three generations went up to write messages of love and goodbye for him in felt tip on his cardboard coffin. It was very moving and there were lots of laughs through the tears.

Andrew Copson

One grandad wanted his grandchildren to be involved, but none felt able to speak at the funeral, so they each placed one of his many, many hats carefully and tenderly upon the coffin to say goodbye. A humanist funeral celebrates a unique life, uniquely.

Humanist celebrant Jo Beddington

As you know, Jen was a great lover of Radio 4 – but not of 'Humphreys', whom she deemed rude. She enjoyed the absurd puns of *I'm Sorry I Haven't a Clue* but also mines of information such as *A History of the World in 100 Objects*. So, based on the memories of Vanessa and Judith, I am now going to channel Neil McGregor for a few minutes and give you the life of Jennifer Knox in 12 objects. With each object will come memories and reasons.

From a ceremony by humanist celebrant Felicity Harvest

Item one: a large plastic bag

Item two is a pair of secateurs

Item three is a spirit level

Item four is a pack of paper handkerchiefs

Item five is a cork

Item six is a pair of corduroy trousers

Item six-and-a half is a lipstick

Item seven, of course, is a teaspoon

Item eight is a Kindle

Item nine is a CD

Item ten is a box of matches

Item eleven is a tennis ball

Item twelve is a packet of Embassy Number 10.

Human funerary practices began with simple 'necrophoresis' – removing the dead, slipping them into fissures or pushing them into the back of rock shelters; sometimes scooping out a hollow, laying plants over them to cover them up. Then there was burial, with beads and ochre. Then there was all manner of things, from cannibalism to cremation, mummification to excarnation, burials with beakers and graves with chariots. And now, we're back looking at necrophoresis again: disappearing the physical remains of the dead, and instead, keeping their memory alive.

Alice Roberts

Bernie liked fashion. In the eighties and nineties, he'd worked in the Covent Garden store of one of the UK's most successful menswear designers and sartorially he was always very particular. He liked to look dapper. We knew that we needed a collective gesture to reflect that, as well as the love and support of all his friends.

As his friends arrived at the ceremony, they found on their chairs luggage labels attached to brightly coloured ribbons, with a note asking them to write to Bernie a personal, heartfelt message. Later in the ceremony, the ribbons were laid in strips over Bernie's willow coffin, creating a beautiful blanket of colour and texture, with all the words from his friends nestled amongst them. They stayed with him throughout the ceremony.

Humanist celebrant Deborah Hooper

When a good friend of mine knew she was dying she told me about a ceremony she had learnt about when on a charity walk in Peru. The idea is that a small fire is started and loved ones gather around it, there are as many logs as there were years that the deceased had been alive. Each log is given to a different friend or family member. They take it in turns to place the log on the fire and share an anecdote or memory, as the memories are shared so the fire grows.

She asked me to make sure this ritual took place in her honour, and she encouraged me to ask for memories and stories from the sublime to the ridiculous. By the end of the evening, not only were we warmed by the literal heat of a fire thirty-seven logs strong, but from the revelling and laughter created as such a ritual took place. It was tremendous.

Humanist celebrant Zena Birch

Saying goodbye

Sometimes mourners design funeral ceremonies without a moment to say goodbye. In my experience, that is frustrating because you leave feeling that something is missing.

Humanist celebrant Hester Brown

The tradition with funerals has been to see the coffin physically depart and this brings a sort of certainty and closure. At burials, whether in cemeteries or natural and woodland burials, the coffin is lowered into the earth in a gesture with obvious symbolism. At crematoria the coffin may also be removed from sight. It may roll beyond a small door, be hidden by curtains, or be lowered into another floor.

Very often now the coffin (or ashes at an ashes-centred ceremony) remains through to the end but it is still possible to say goodbye within the ceremony. In many humanist ceremonies the celebrants will address these words to the dead person, but sometimes mourners may like to say words of love and remembrance together.

John,

With admiration, respect and appreciation, we've remembered your life and the unique, unforgettable, and irreplaceable person you have been.

Thank you for your empathy, your friendship, your love.

Thank you for your musicality, your inspiration, your talent, your vision.

You have touched everyone you encountered with your kindness, your patience and your generosity.

Your time with us was too short, and you still had much to give, but we are so grateful that you were a part of our lives.

From a ceremony by humanist celebrant Deborah Hooper

Beloved grandmother, mother, sister, and friend to many, we commit your body to the earth.

Rest in the hearts and minds of all you love, and all who love you.

Birth is a beginning and death a destination;

But life is a journey.

A going – a growing, from stage to stage:

From childhood to maturity and youth to old age.

From innocence to awareness and ignorance to knowing;

From foolishness to discretion

and then perhaps, to wisdom.

From a ceremony by humanist celebrant Karen Lewis

Together we have remembered Margaret and marked her special presence in the world.

You have committed her memory to your hearts to remember for always.

Now, in this beautiful place, with enduring love, we commit her body to the earth.

She will be part of this place through the warmth of summer and the clear air of winter; through the new growth of spring and the mists of autumn.

From a ceremony by humanist celebrant Jenny Lloyd

Robert, as we come to the time for goodbyes,

Part of our grief may be regret

For things done or left undone,

Words said, or never said,

Or moments that never happened.

This is the time to lay aside these regrets.

We respect your journey through life,

A journey which is now ended.

From a ceremony by humanist celebrant
Felicity Harvest

The celebration of Jennifer's life is complete. It's time to say our final farewell. This may be difficult, but it is important, as our focus is on the circle of life as we commit her body to the earth. This wildlife sanctuary will be her final resting place. Here a hazel tree will be planted when the season allows, and she will become one with the woodland. Not only does this support this wonderful space as a gift to future generations, but it is also a beautiful place for you to visit, to reflect and to remember her in peace.

From a ceremony by humanist celebrant Karen Lewis

Julia, with love and respect we let you go, and release your body to its final transformation back to the elements of the world. Julia will live on in the lives and memories of those she has known and those who have known her. Her energy survives too, for we know that energy never gets created or destroyed but rather transformed. So you might, if you wish, imagine her energy in the beat of a bird's wing as it flies across these fields or perhaps in the rustle of leaves in this orchard – waves crashing on a beach or perhaps in the rush of water in a river.

From an orchard burial by humanist celebrant Peter Gaskin

Thank you all for being here today.
As you return to your own lives,
enriched by your memories of him,
please go gently, be kind and live
your lives well.

From a ceremony by humanist celebrant Karen Lewis

With thanks to . . .

Mike Ashbridge

Sue Baumbach

Jo Beddington

Jane Blackman

Hester Brown

Ruth Brown Shepherd

Jenny Bullough

Adele Chaplin

Natalie Charles

Chris Dean

Susan Dobinson

Dylan Edwards

Peter Gaskin

Val Hart

Mandy Hagan

Felicity Harvest

Celia Hickson

Stewart Holden

Bob Kiddle

Hilary Leighter

Karen Lewis

Jenny Lloyd

Ewan Main

Mary McEntegart

Gitte Monis

Joanna Mutlow

Kate Owens-Palmer

Nicholas Pinegar

Maggie Platts

Susannah Read

Sara Scott

Lisa Sharpe

Viv Thomas

Gary Vaudin

Sue Walder

Graeme Ward

Copyright and references

pp.17 Kathryn Mannix, *With the End in Mind* (HarperCollins 2018); 19 William Shakespeare, *The Tempest*, Act IV Scene 1; 21 Lucretius, tr. A.E. Stallings, *The Nature of Things* (Penguin Classics 2007); 23 WK Clifford's epitaph; 27 E.M. Forster, *Howards End* (Penguin Classics 2000); 28 Ursula K. Le Guin, *A Wizard of Earthsea* (Gollancz 2019); 29 Marcus Aurelius, tr. Martin Hammond, *Meditations* (Penguin Classics 2006); 31 Richard Holloway, *Looking in the Distance* (Canongate 2004); 33 (top) Clive James, *Sentenced to Life* (Picador 2015), (bottom) *Selected Works of Jawaharlal Nehru, Second Series: Volume 15: Part II*, ed. S. Gopal (Oxford University Press 1994); 35 Stephen Fry, *Moab is my Washpot* (Cornerstone 2004); 39 'David Attenborough: "I'm an essential evil"', *Guardian* 21 Oct 2011; 41 Danusha Laméris, 'Feeding the Worms', *Bonfire Opera* (University of Pittsburgh Press 2020); 43 Epictetus, tr. Robert Dobbin, *Discourses and Selected Writings* (Penguin Classics 2018); 45 W.D. Hamilton, 'My intended burial and why', *Ethology Ecology and Evolution* 12(2): 111–122 (2000); 49 A. Powell Davies, *The Language of the Heart* (Lindsey Press 1956); 51 Terry Pratchett,

Reaper Man (Corgi 2012); 53 'Where Do the Dead Go in Our Imaginations?', *New York Times* 6 Mar 2021; 56–7 Merrit Malloy, 'Epitaph', *My Song for Him Who Never Sang to Me* (Crown 1975); 59 'Helen Dunmore: facing mortality and what we leave behind', *Guardian* 4 Mar 2017; 60 *The Note-Books of Samuel Butler*, ed. Henry Festing Jones (A.C. Fifield 1912); 65 Herbert Read, *The Contrary Experience* (Faber 1963); 66 'One Foot Before the Other', Frank Turner, Xtra Mile 2011; 67 John Donne, *Devotions Upon Emergent Occasions* (University of Michigan Press 1959); 68 Roger McGough, 'Everything Touches, *Sensational!* (Macmillan 2005); 71 James Hemming, *Individual Morality* (Nelson 1969); 72–3 *Forces of Nature* episode 2, 11 Jul 2016; 74–5 Kurt Vonnegut, *Slaughterhouse-Five* (Vintage 2000); 79 Philip Pullman, *The Amber Spyglass* (Scholastic 2000); 81 Walt Whitman, 'Warm Summer Sun', *The Complete Poems* (Penguin Classics 2004); 82 'The Joy of Living', Ewan MacColl and Peggy Seeger, 1986; 83 Zora Neale Hurston, *Dust Tracks on a Road* (Virago Modern Classics 2020); 84–5 Thomas Hardy, 'Transformations', *Selected Poems* (Penguin Classics 1993); 87 'The Water', Johnny Flynn and Laura Marling, Transgressive Records 2010; 88 *Wonders of the Universe* episode 1, 6 Mar 2011; 91 George Orwell, *Essays* (Penguin Modern Classics 2000); 93 Alfred, Lord Tennyson, *In Memoriam* (Edward Moxon 1850);

95 'The day the sky fell in', *Guardian* 3 Dec 2005;
96–7 'The last word on Sorrow' *Guardian* 16 Oct
1999; 98–9 'Janet Ellis shares her experience of
coping with grief and isolation during lockdown',
Good Thinking & Humanists UK YouTube video
youtube/AieHvXea19g, 25 Feb 2021; 100 'Natural
wonder: David Attenborough on facing his
mortality', *New Zealand Herald* 2 Dec 2016;
101 Julian Barnes, *Flaubert's Parrot* (Vintage 2009);
103 Clare Harner, 'Immortality', *The Gypsy* Dec
1934; 105 Helen Lowrie Marshall, 'Afterglow',
Close to the Heart (Doubleday 1958); 115 *Objections
to Humanism*, ed. H.J. Blackham (Pelican 1965);
123 Char March, 'Still', *The Thousand Natural Shocks*
(Indigo Dreams Publishing 2011); 125 The Bertrand
Russell Peace Foundation Ltd; 127 Stevie Smith,
'When One', *Selected Poems* (Penguin Modern
Classics 2002); 128 Hermann Hesse, tr. James
Wright, 'Going to Sleep', *Poems* (Jonathan Cape
1977); 129 Rabindranath Tagore, *Farewell My Friend
and The Garden* (Jaico Books 1966); 131 'The last
word on Death', *Guardian* 20 Jan 2001; 134 Viktor E.
Frankl, *The Doctor and the Soul* (Souvenir Press 2004);
135 Cecil Day Lewis, 'A Time to Dance', *A Time to
Dance and Other Poems* (Hogarth Press 1935);
136 Mary Yarnall, 'Too Soon' (Chelsea House 1955);
138 Stephanie Paige Cole, *Still* (Strategic 2013);

142–3 Char March, 'We Were Parents', *The Thousand Natural Shocks*; 147 'Ram Dass on self-judgment', www.ramdass.org/ram-dass-on-self-judgement; 151 Richard Eyre, *Utopia and Other Places* (Bloomsbury 1996); 152–3 Clare Jones, 'As We Look Back'; 154 *The Collected Stories of Colette* (Vintage 2003); 155 Rowan Coleman, *We Are All Made of Stars* (Ebury 2016); 175 William Shakespeare, *Macbeth*, Act IV Scene 3

All images via iStock

The Good Funeral Guide is a social enterprise dedicated to supporting, empowering and representing the interests of dying and bereaved people.

Wholly independent of the funeral industry, they promote the importance of funerals and the transformative power that a truly personal funeral ceremony can have.

www.goodfuneralguide.co.uk

You can find a celebrant who will help you plan your funeral while you are still alive.

More and more humanist celebrants are offering this service and you can search online for one near you.

www.humanists.uk/ceremonies

Humanists UK

At Humanists UK, we want a tolerant world where rational thinking and kindness prevail. We work to support lasting change for a better society, championing ideas for the one life we have, drawing on contemporary humanist thought and the worldwide humanist tradition.

Our work helps people to be happier and more fulfilled, and by bringing non-religious people together we help them develop their own views and an understanding of the world around them.

We're committed to putting humanism into practice. Through our ceremonies, pastoral support, education services, and campaigning work, we advance free thinking and freedom of choice so everyone can live in a fair and equal society.

Since 1896, we've always been a growing movement at the forefront of social change. If you want to support us in our work, please do join or donate. We are dependent on charitable giving to continue our work.

Find out more at our website, at humanists.uk.

Humanists UK, 39 Moreland Street, London EC1V 8BB. Registered charity in England and Wales no. 285987 and company limited by guarantee no. 228781.